T0195690

Where He Leads

AN IN-DEPTH LOOK AT THE 23RD PSALM

Adiya Adams

WESTBOW
PRESS®
A DIVISION OF THOMAS NELSON
& ZONDERVAN

WestBow Press books may be ordered through booksellers or by contacting:

WestBow Press
A Division of Thomas Nelson & Zondervan
1663 Liberty Drive
Bloomington, IN 47403
www.westbowpress.com
844-714-3454

Unless marked otherwise, all scripture quotations are taken from the King James Version.

Scripture quotations marked AMP are taken from the Amplified® Bible, Copyright © 2015 by The Lockman Foundation. Used by permission.

ISBN: 978-1-6642-7908-7 (sc)
ISBN: 978-1-6642-7909-4 (e)

Library of Congress Control Number: 2022917753

Print information available on the last page.

WestBow Press rev. date: 11/15/2022

Contents

This book is dedicated to the LORD who is my Shepherd.

I thank God for my family whom He has used to sharpen and encourage me throughout this journey of faith.

Introduction

In John Chapter 10, Jesus refers to Himself as the Good Shepherd. He shows the contrast between the Good Shepherd and the hireling, who does not care for the sheep at all.[1]

Not many understand what the work of a shepherd is, especially those born and raised in the city. We all know the shepherd looks after the sheep, but there are unique characteristics that mark the shepherd and his sheep.

For starters, sheep do not think for themselves; they simply follow. They go wherever the shepherd wants them to go. This is where the saying "following like sheep" originates. That phrase is nearly always meant to be derogatory as it intimates that the sheep is mindless.

However, we are going to take an in-depth look at the twenty-third psalm, and we will see that being a sheep does not mean someone is mindless; in fact, sheep are very mindful of who they follow.

---

[1] See John 10:11–12

It was David, the sweet psalmist of Israel, who wrote the twenty-third psalm. We are told in 1 Samuel that he was the youngest of eight sons and he kept sheep, which means he was a shepherd. When David wrote this psalm, he knew what he was talking about. He understood his responsibility to the sheep and his sheep's dependency on him. Even though it was David who wrote the psalm, as believers in Jesus Christ, this is God's Word to us, and we have every right to apply it to our own lives.

There are only six verses to this psalm, but each verse speaks to us in a unique way that increases our confidence in God and makes us lift our eyes to Him as we walk in the path where He leads us.

I pray as you read this book that, like the Bereans, you will search the Scriptures and that the Lord will reveal His will and purpose for you even as He molds you into the image of His dear Son and our Savior Jesus Christ.

THE RELATIONSHIP:
HIS OWNERSHIP

The LORD *is my Shepherd; I shall not want.*

—PSALM 23:1

The psalmist here affirms God's ownership of him. LORD is God's name. That means Yahweh, the I AM. We see the first use of that name in Exodus 3:14, when God tells Moses to tell the children of Israel that the I AM had sent him to them. David here acknowledges God's sovereignty and power as well as His ownership of him. The LORD is not just any shepherd but David's own Shepherd.

This verse establishes the relationship between shepherd and sheep. The sheep belong to the Shepherd, who is the LORD. As believers in Christ, we belong to the LORD.[2] Jesus Himself calls us His sheep in John 10:16. Psalm 23:1 demonstrates David's confidence

---

[2] See 1 Corinthians 3:23

in God as His keeper. The relationship is personal. David calls Him "my" Shepherd—not somebody else's, but his. Do we have that personal relationship with God through Jesus Christ to boldly call Him "my Father" just as Jesus taught us to in the Lord's Prayer? Do we approach His throne of grace with the mindset that we are approaching our Father's throne, and are confident of Him answering our prayer? The LORD longs to have that personal relationship with each of His children.[3]

Confessing and affirming that he is the sheep shows humility on David's part. Like the sheep that simply go where the shepherd leads, the will of the Master has become David's will. As Christians, we are told, "Humble yourselves therefore under the mighty Hand of God that He may exalt you in due time" (1 Peter 5:6).

We need to submit our wills to His to continue in that intimate relationship with Christ and for God to lead us in His own paths of righteousness.

Paul exhorted the Philippians,

> Let this mind be in you, which was also in Christ Jesus: Who being in the form of God, thought it not robbery to be equal with God: but made Himself of no reputation, and took upon Him the form of a servant, and was made in the likeness of men: and being found in fashion as a man, He humbled Himself and became obedient unto death, even the death of the cross. (Philippians 2:5–8)

---

[3] See John 14:23

Christ submitted Himself totally to the Father, and He was highly exalted and given a name that is above every other name.[4] That name is our rock, the name by which we have our authority, and the name in which we stand as believers and rebuke the enemy because he has been defeated.

Jesus is our example. If we are to please God, we must walk just as He walked. Jesus always told His listeners that whatever He did and whatever He said was according to the Father's will.[5] Like Jesus, we must submit our wills to the Father's for Him to be able to work His will in our lives, and our Father's will is always perfect.

OUR SURRENDER

Sheep do not think for themselves; they depend on the Shepherd's directions and trust His decisions for them. We sometimes doubt God's purpose for us, but He has said that His thoughts toward us are "continually of peace and not of evil" (Jeremiah 29:11).

The purpose is to give us that which we look to Him for.

However, if we are honest with ourselves, we know we do not always act as if that is true—that God's purpose in every aspect of our lives is to do us good. The minute something goes wrong in our lives, we start to doubt His faithfulness to us. Doubting God is a serious issue because we are questioning His integrity. He has given us His Word and has also promised,

> For as the rain cometh down from and the snow from heave, and returneth not hither, but watereth the

---

[4] See Philippians 2:9–11
[5] See John 6:38 and John 12:49–50

earth, and maketh it bring forth and bud, that it may give seed to the sower, and bread to the eater: so shall My word be that goeth forth out of My mouth: it shall not return unto me void, but it shall accomplish that which I please, and it shall prosper in the thing whereto I sent it. (Isaiah 55:10–11)

This means that no matter what, that which God has spoken will surely be fulfilled. He holds up everything by the word of His power. Everything in the entire universe is upheld by Him.

Scientists talk about "dark matter." *Dark* means unexplainable or undetectable. They realized that galaxies do not move and behave without the existence of some unseen and unexplainable gravitational force that they term "dark matter." The answer is so simple. Jesus upholds all things by the word of His power. According to the book of Hebrews, God

hath in these last days spoken unto us by His Son, Whom He hath appointed heir of all things, by Whom also He made the worlds; Who being the brightness of His glory and the express image of His Person, and upholding all things by the word of His power, when He had by Himself purged our sins, sat down on the right hand of the Majesty on high. (Hebrews 1:1–3)

Sometimes we become very impatient as we wait for God's will to unfold in our lives. We are exhorted in James 1 to hold on to our faith in patience. The verse reads, "But let patience have her perfect work, that ye may be perfect and entire, wanting nothing" (James 1:4).

In chapter 5 of this same book, we are reminded of the patience of Job: "Ye have heard of the patience of Job and have seen the end of the Lord; that the Lord is very pitiful, and of tender mercy" (James 5:11).

This verse assures us that no matter the trials we face (and all of us do), we can rest patiently in the Lord, knowing that He is in control and will bring His perfect will to pass when we leave it all to Him.

Recently I attended a women's conference at Calvary Chapel Awaken Church in Las Vegas. The main speaker exhorted us to write down the things that we were trusting God for and leave the list at the altar. There were things that I had been trusting God for; like most of us, sometimes I would check on God to see how He was doing with those issues and question why it was taking so long. Now I remind myself that I have given it to Him and that He is in absolute control. We need to totally abandon every issue and every situation that only He can resolve to Him. Leave them at the altar, whether you write them down or not. (Writing things down does help.) And once you have given them to Him, trust Him for that "expected end."

We trust Him, because "without faith, it is impossible to please God" (Hebrews 11:6).

We have to be totally persuaded in our hearts that God is working out everything for our good. Being patient ensures that God's perfect will would be done in our lives.

"I shall not want" is a very bold statement. It is total confidence in the Shepherd's ability and willingness to provide for His sheep. No matter what his needs are, the psalmist is confident that the Lord will supply all of them without fail. Philippians 4:19 tells us the same thing because Jesus Christ is "the same yesterday, and today, and forever" (Hebrews 13:8).

As long as the Lord is our Shepherd, all our needs will be met because of Christ and because we have believed in the only begotten Son of God.

Romans 8:32 assures us that since God spared not Jesus Christ but gave Him up to die for us, He will also give us all things that we need because of Him. God wants us to know that giving Jesus up to die for us should be proof enough that He is ready, willing, and able to meet our every other need. Jesus buttresses this fact in the book of Matthew when He says, "Seek ye first the kingdom of God and His righteousness; and all these things shall be added to you" (Matthew 6:33).

Chapter Two

THE BLESSINGS

He maketh me to lie down in green pastures:
He leadeth me beside the still waters.

—PSALM 23:2

Having affirmed God's sovereignty in his life and his confidence in Him as His Shepherd, the psalmist goes on to enumerate all the blessings that follow him as a result of this wonderful relationship. He lists all that the Shepherd does that makes him never lack any good thing.

GREEN PASTURES

Pastures are for grazing. The sheep eat small quantities of grass at a time until they are full. The Shepherd takes His sheep only where the pasture is green, where there is constant water and the grass is never dry but remains green and gives a sweet taste. Jesus, our Shepherd, leads us only to green, constantly watered pastures: His Word. We need to graze on the Word daily. Job said, "I have esteemed the words of His mouth more than my necessary food" (Job 23:11).

The Word of God meant more to Job than the food that was necessary to sustain him.[6] If in our Christian lives we have spiritual dryness, it is not the Lord's fault because He has given us everything to keep us constantly watered. It could be that we are not following where He is leading or we might be grazing in the wrong pasture.

Were the sheep to turn from following their shepherd and graze on another pasture they think might be good for them, that could spell danger for them. It is the shepherd who knows the good grass, where there are no wild animals, and where danger is least.

The Word of God is always green. It waters us and brings refreshment to our souls when we read it daily and apply it to our lives. We all know the power of a cold glass of water to quench our thirst. Oh the sigh of satisfaction when that cool liquid flows down our throats. It is so refreshing, and it brings such relief from the heat and sweat that have hitherto been endured. The Word of God does that to our souls. When we are all heated up with the vicissitudes of life, it is the Word that brings us the peace we yearn for, even as we put all our trust in the Word.

In our walk with Jesus, we might sometimes spy certain pastures that look greener than the one the Lord is leading us to, and we might want to stop and graze instead of continuing to follow the Lord's leading. Some of us can testify to that happening in our lives. We find ourselves in situations that we know deep in our hearts are not where we should be, that do not allow us to conform to God's

---

[6] See also Psalm 119:103

Word. Nevertheless, we linger anyway and continue to graze because everything looks just as green and the grass tastes so sweet. *Can the Lord do any better?* is our voiceless question and the answer is yes, He can. He knows the quality of every grass in the field because He is the Omniscient One.

However, in our walk with the Lord, we sometimes get in a toxic situation with our eyes wide open thinking things might turn out differently; but it only leaves us crying out for help from Him. He always hears our cry, but oh the wounds and pain we endure because of our disobedience in not following Him all the way.

We read books and watch movies that we know instinctively will do us not good but harm, yet we continue to read and watch anyway.

We knowingly engage in behaviors that do not glorify Christ at all, but we continue in them anyway citing the grace of God that is so real and powerful. But the Word says, "All things are lawful for me but all things are not expedient" (1 Corinthians 10:23).

Which means we should not take the grace of God in vain . We should not "continue in sin so that grace may abound", like Paul said in Romans 5:1.

The Lord knows which grass is toxic, which one feeds from contaminated waters, and which would cause disease to His sheep. That is why we need to hear His voice calling to us through His Word. He says:

> "Verily, verily, I say unto you, he that entereth not by the door into the sheepfold, but climbeth up some other way, the same is a thief and a robber. But He that entereth in by the door is the Shepherd of the sheep. To Him the porter openeth; and the sheep hear

His voice: and He calleth His own sheep by name, and leadeth them out." (John 10:1–3)

We really need to listen to and obey the voice of our Shepherd.

The shepherd also knows how deep the water table runs in every pasture, and our Shepherd leads us to the best: His Word, the still waters that not only run deep but also bring peace and comfort to us. This is what makes Jesus the Good Shepherd who cares so much for His sheep that He was even willing to give His life up for us. We must hear and obey His voice.

You know the relationship you are in is just wrong, and maybe the Lord has even spoken to you about it, but you continue in it anyway. Maybe God gave you a check in your spirit about that incredible job offer that would likely solve all your problems; you accepted the job anyway, only to find yourself in a compromised situation, obligated to do things that are contrary to the Word of God. What do you do then? You are already grazing, but then you realize that this is not the Lord's green pasture. It was only a mirage. You are still hungry, you feel weak, sometimes even sick and ready to give up. You might rationalize like this: "How could it be so wrong? I'm grazing here but I have my eyes on the pasture where the other sheep are. They look about the same to me. My wife and children are happy, and we have everything we need. My children go to the best schools. Without that expensive operation, my son could have died. So how could my being unequally yoked in business be so wrong?" Maybe your rationalization is like this: "This guy loves me and does everything for me even though he is married. My children love him, and I cannot stand for them to lose another father figure in their lives. Is it wrong to want happiness for my kids?" Maybe your rationalization is like this: "I know X is not a Christian, and the crowd she runs with is really wild, but as long as I do not do all the things they do, it is okay for me to continue to hang out with them"

The fact, dear reader, is that the devil is "the god of this world" (2 Corinthians 4:4). He rules over this world. His rule is legitimate because Adam handed power over to him in the Garden of Eden when he Adam disobeyed God and obeyed the devil. Adam had been created by God to rule over all the earth[7] while God ruled over him, but Adam made himself a servant of the devil through his disobedience to God.[8] Jesus Christ came as the second Adam in perfect obedience to God to redeem us from that bondage of sin and of death which the first Adam had put us under through his disobedience.[9] Jesus is the Son of God but He became a Man for the purpose of redemption and was perfectly obedient to the Father.[10] Thus He bought us back to our Father God through His death on the cross and His resurrection from the dead in power on the third day. We need to acknowledge our sinfulness in the sight of God and receive His gift of salvation through Jesus Christ.

By obedience to the Word of God, according to Romans 10:9, the one who believes he obtains salvation through Jesus Christ, the Son of God, has been "translated…from the power of darkness into the Kingdom of His dear Son" (Colossians 1:13) Jesus Christ and is no longer under the devil's rule. The Bible tells us that "All that is in the world, the lust of the flesh, and the lust of the eyes and the pride of life is not of the Father" (1 John 2:15–17).

---

[7] See Genesis 1:28

[8] See Romans 6:16

[9] See 1 Corinthians 15:45

[10] See Romans 5:18–19

So even though believers in Jesus Christ are still in the world, we do not belong to this world.[11] We belong to the Kingdom of God.[12] This does not mean that we stop obeying our governments. We obey our civic rulers as long as we honor the Word of God. But we do have our own God-given will to exercise.

Christ our Shepherd makes us lie down in green pastures, pastures that are continually watered. He knows the way to such pastures, and we need to trust Him to guide us to those pastures. We need to follow Him all the way through and not stop by the wayside to nibble at seemingly green grass.

Proverbs Chapter 5 talks about the "strange woman" who lures men to their death. Of course, death is not written on her forehead; all that the victims see is the promise of pleasure, delight, and fulfilled heart's desires. She looks warm and inviting, dripping with sweetness like the seemingly green grass. However, the Bible says that seeming sweetness is actually wormwood, and that her house is a house of destruction that is a one-way ticket to hell. We are cautioned to avoid such at all costs. "Stolen waters are sweet" (Proverbs 9:17), but what comes after you've enjoyed the sweetness? Death and hell.[13]

There are so many voices in the world all claiming to have the answer. This causes confusion for a lot of people, and they tend to listen to the wrong voices. If you are a believer in Christ and you have the Holy Spirit dwelling in you, the Bible says we should "Believe not every spirit, but try the spirits whether they are of God: because many false prophets are gone out into the world" (1 John 4:1).

This should be our test, and anything that does not line up with

---

[11] John 17:16; Romans 12:2

[12] Luke 11:20; Luke 17:20

[13] See Proverbs 9:17–18

the Word of God should be put aside. Everything we hear, believe, and practice should be according to the Word of God. If some doctrine sounds very close to the Truth but is not supported by the Word, it is not of God. Jesus tells us very plainly that the Holy Spirit who is the Spirit of Truth will reveal the Truth in our hearts. He will never tell us anything that is outside the Word of God.[14]

We see our absolute need to know the Word of God, for this is how we can compare what is true and what is false.

We need to be patient as we follow the Lord our Shepherd as He leads to His pastures. He is faithful who promised us life and blessings. He makes everything beautiful in His time. Even though the journey may seem long and arduous (and the Lord did promise us tribulations together with salvation), He will take us to where He wants us to be.[15]

FRUITFULNESS

The Word of life brings greenness to our lives here on earth. Greenness shows the fruitfulness of God in our lives.[16] Psalm 1 says the godly person "shall be like a tree planted by the rivers of water, that bringeth forth his fruit in his season; his leaf also shall not wither and whatsoever he doeth shall prosper" (Psalm 1:3). It is not that there are no storms or scorching heat or heavy rains or other disturbances to the tree, but that tree is planted firmly in rivers of water and it keeps bearing fruit despite all odds.

So should we, as children of God, be fruit bearing. Others should

---

[14] See John 16:13
[15] See Jeremiah 29:11
[16] Psalm 92:12–15

see Jesus in our lives. In our words and in our actions, the Lord should be glorified always, in spite of difficulties and oppressions. Is this hard to do? Yes, if you do it on your own, in your own strength. However, it is the Holy Spirit who enables us to live a Christ like, Christ portraying, Christ filled life. That is what He is doing in the world right now: glorifying Christ, whether in the heart of the unbeliever through conviction of sin, righteousness and judgment, or in the heart of a child of God confirming the promises of God and guiding our hearts into His will. We then need to surrender our all to the Lord so He can work His perfect will in us.[17]

If we say He is our Shepherd and we are His sheep, we must follow His footsteps, walking even as He walked. May our heart's cry always be to be more like Him every day.

STILL WATERS

The second part of verse 2 says that He leads His sheep beside still waters. This is the water the Shepherd leads us to quench our thirst. It is His Holy Spirit through His Word who quenches our thirst for God and His righteousness. Hence, we are exhorted in 1Thessalonians to "Quench not the Spirit" (1 Thessalonians 5:19).

We should allow the Spirit of God to lead us into His will. We should not resist Him when He is speaking to us, but be obedient; otherwise, we might not be able to hear Him anymore. That is not a place any Christian should be. The Bible calls that state of not hearing the Spirit's voice a "seared conscience."

---

[17] See John 16:7–15

Still water has no tide or current and very slight incline. This means there is no outside pressure or force exerted on it to change its structure. No external force or power can change our position in Christ, nor can anything separate us from His Love.[18]

There is also normally a lot more going on in the still water that can be discerned, hence the stillness. We can never fathom the depths of God's love for us. It is too awful and too deep, and it will take eternity for us to understand it.[19]

The waters are still because of the peace Jesus our Shepherd gives to us. He told us in John 14:27, "My peace I leave with you." We have peace with the Father because of the sacrifice of Jesus on the cross, and we are brought into a relationship with Him as His children.[20] Jesus brings peace into our souls: peace from anxiety, worries, the cares of this world, and anything else that might cause our souls not to be at peace. We have peace knowing He is leading, and He will never fail us or forsake us.

When there was a storm raging and threatening His disciples (Mark 4:36–41), all He said was "Peace be still" (Mark 4:39) and there was calm. It is that same calmness that our Shepherd wants us to have in our souls even as we trust Him and follow Him.

There are no jagged rocks or torrents in still waters, so we need not be afraid of being swept away by the tide, being hurt by rocks, or slipping from a steep slope. We are standing on the Rock that cannot be moved, so we cannot be moved either. Jesus is perfect. His sacrifice was perfect, and His Word is perfect. In His Word, we

---

[18] See Romans 8:36

[19] 1 John 3:1; John 3:16; Jeremiah 31:3

[20] John 1:12

have everything we need for "life and godliness" (2 Peter 1:3), and everything we need to go through life victoriously.[21] May we always trust our Lord and Savior for direction and guidance in every aspect of our lives.

---

[21] See 2 Peter 1:2–4

HIS RIGHTEOUSNESS

He restoreth my soul; He leadeth me in the paths
of righteousness for His Name's sake.

—PSALM 23:3

RESTORATION

If there were no buffetings, no trials, no temptations, and no hardships, then there would be no need for any restoration of the soul. But these are all things we face, sometimes on a daily basis, and they affect our souls. This is actually part of the salvation package from God. Jesus told us that we would receive a hundredfold blessing of all we have given up for Him. We would also receive persecution and "in the world to come, eternal life" (Mark 10:29–31). God allows all these trials to come our way because He knows He is well able to restore us. We become stronger as we go through trials and emerge victorious in Jesus's Name. Then we are strengthened even more and are able to withstand the enemy if he comes around again. We are also able to encourage others because we have walked in those very same shoes.[22]

Are we weary, discouraged, and almost ready to give up? The Shepherd leads us in those paths where we can find comfort and restoration in Him, paths that are marked out in His Word.[23] He restores the peace the enemy has stolen. He restores our joy in Him because that joy brings the strength we need to go on. The knowledge that Jesus is our everything, that He is going through that trial and buffeting with us, brings peace and comfort to our hearts.[24]

Paul's life demonstrated his total dependency on God for restoration. Jesus had already told him that he was going to suffer many things for His sake,[25] and Paul did suffer many things. He testifies that sometimes he was sick almost to the point of death, that sometimes he was in such despair that he felt he was not going to make it.[26] He also testifies that God delivered him from every one of these situations.[27] Paul depended completely on the Lord and so should we. God has promised He will always make a way out for us—not our own way, but His way.[28]

Jesus, our Shepherd, overcame every temptation by the Word of God, as described in Matthew 4:1–11. Likewise, every provision has been made for us in the Word of God to overcome any and every temptation He allows to come our way. He restores our souls.

---

[22] See 2 Corinthians 1:2–5

[23] See Psalm 119:105

[24] See 2 Corinthians 1:5

[25] See Acts 9:15–16

[26] See 2 Corinthians 11:23–29

[27] See 2 Corinthians 6:3–10; 7:5–6; 12:10

[28] See 1 Corinthians 10:13

In 1 Samuel Chapter 30, we are told that David went through a very difficult time. After King Achish refused his request to fight with the Philistines, David and his men returned to their settlement in Ziklag. What a sight met their eyes: Ziklag had been burned down to the ground, and their entire families taken captive. The pain was unbearable. Grown men wept until they had no strength left. Their bitterness led them to resent David for bringing them into this situation, and they spoke of killing him by stoning. These were men who had put their lives on the line for David. They were his men, his comrades; they were under his command and had been through fiery trials together. At that point in time, however, they wanted to get rid of David. Their pain was so great, they could not think clearly. David had to endure the pain of losing his own family, the pain of a leader who has failed those who trusted in him, and the pain of his trusted friends turning against him. Did David give up? No, he did not. Rather the Bible says he "encouraged himself in the Lord." He found strength and restoration in the Lord for his soul's anguish. God, who is the God of all comfort, comforted David and gave him and his men strength to pursue and recover everything taken. They recovered not only what they had lost, but also gained so much more wealth and spoil from their adversaries, the Amalekites.

What have you lost that you need God to restore? Your peace? Your joy? Your commitment to Him? A broken relationship? He can restore all. If you have wandered away from the Shepherd, return, repent, and ask for His restoration.[29]

---

[29] Matthew 7:7

RIGHTEOUSNESS

The LORD restores us to lead us evermore in His paths of righteousness. When we become believers in Christ, we inherit His righteousness, according to Romans 3:21–24. God no longer sees our sin and iniquities; He sees the righteousness of His Son Jesus Christ and He accepts us as His sons and daughters according to Ephesians 1:6. Wherever He leads from henceforth, it is a good path because it is a path of righteousness. Are we fully persuaded that the Lord leads us in His paths of righteousness? Do we follow without question and in absolute faith in His Word?

Even as He leads us in righteousness, revealing Himself to us through His Word, it is for the glory of His Name.[30] He made the promise in Genesis 3:15 that Jesus would be the Deliverer of mankind and His Word cannot be broken. He always fulfills it to the praise of His glory.

Jesus has already died for mankind and has risen again. Now we have to acknowledge that sacrifice personally in our lives. If we, as believers, realize that we are not walking in that righteousness that Jesus came to bestow upon us, we need to repent and go back to following the Shepherd.

---

[30] See Ephesians 1:6

Chapter Four

HIS PROTECTION

Yea though I walk through the valley of the shadow
of death, I will fear no evil: for Thou art with me;
Thy rod and Thy staff they comfort me.

—PSALM 23:4

TRIALS AND TEMPTATIONS

In this verse, the psalmist continues to express his confidence in the
LORD His Shepherd, even in the midst of danger.

There are some things to observe here. First of all, this verse
demonstrates walking through experience. His experience of adversity
is not permanent. He looks ahead to the time when he will no longer
be in such a situation. This kind of attitude represents faith in God's
Word.[31] He walks through danger and difficulties with confidence,

---

[31] Hebrews 11:6

knowing that the Lord is right there with him because He promises to never leave or forsake him. God will *never* leave His children in the midst of trouble, even if He is the One who allowed it. We should also have hope that no matter the challenges facing us, God is faithful and will bring us out of it. There is always a purpose for God allowing us to endure fiery trials. He told the Israelites that He wanted to humble them and prove them.[32] He also wanted to let them know that His Word was sufficient for them.[33] We need to know the lessons God wants us to learn from the trials He allows to come our way, and to rest assured that He will definitely make a way out for us.

The second thing we have to observe is that the psalmist calls this place "the valley of the shadow of death" not the valley of death. Death overshadows that valley, but that is all it does: overshadow. It is a threat that cannot be realized because the Shepherd is the One leading the way. Jesus conquered sin and death on the cross and He declared, "It is finished" (John 19:30). From then on, all who trust in Jesus Christ are nestled in the secret place of the Most High under the shadow of the Almighty.[34] God has you hidden in a safe place where you cannot be found by the enemy. As you go through this valley, with all sorts of dangers threatening you, know that you are safe and "your life is hid with Christ in God" (Colossians 3:3). May we have the deep, unwavering assurance in our hearts that as we walk through the valley of life with its loneliness, fears, anxieties, trials, and temptations, we are not alone. It might seem sometimes that God is giving you more than you are able to bear, but He is not.

---

[32] See Deuteronomy 8:2

[33] See Deuteronomy 8:3

[34] Psalm 91:1

One family member said to me, "I'm not Job. I'm not Moses. This is too much." This referred to the pain he endures everyday as a result of sickle cell disease. Sometimes, like Job, we just cannot fathom why God allows certain situations, but one thing we should know is that we are not alone. The Lord is always there, and if He allowed a situation that seems unbearable to occur, it is because He knows that He is able to deliver us completely. He assures:

> No temptation (regardless of its source) has overtaken or enticed you that is not common to human experience (nor is any temptation unusual or beyond human resistance); but God is faithful (to His Word—He is compassionate and trustworthy), and He will not let you be tempted beyond your ability (to resist), but along with the temptation He (has in the past and is now and) will (always) provide the way out as well, so that you will be able to endure it (without yielding, and will overcome temptation with joy). (1 Corinthians 10:13 AMP)

That was the psalmist's reason for fearing no evil: "for Thou art with me." He had the assurance in his heart that he was not alone.

The psalmist's confession and comfort was not only based on the fact that the LORD was with him; the LORD also had weapons that could be used to defend him, namely His rod and His staff. A shepherd, in those days, always carried a rod and a staff. The rod was a symbol of the shepherd's authority. It looks rather like the rod Moses carried in the 1956 film *The Ten Commandments*. The staff was like the rod but with a crook. Both were used in the defense and direction of the sheep. Sheep are more liable to wander from the flock and thus become prey to wild animals. The shepherd used his staff to guide the sheep and also gently but firmly pull back into the fold those who may have wandered away. The rod was used to defend the sheep from attackers, to count the sheep, and prod them along through the pastures and eventually back to the sheepfold.

The rod and staff God uses to prod us, guide us, and pull us back into His fold if we stray is His Word. This is the Word that lights our path so we can see clearly the way we are to go. It even acts as a lamp at our feet so that our every step is illuminated and our feet do not slip.[35] This was a source of comfort to the psalmist.

In Psalm 119 verse 49, the psalmist reminds God of His Word, upon which he had put his hope. That is what God wants us to do: take His Word back to Him and remind Him of His promises to us.[36] It is quite okay to put the Lord in remembrance of His Word to us when we find ourselves in difficult or impossible situations. Hezekiah did just that. God heard him and added fifteen years to his life.[37] Hezekiah reminded God that he was walking before Him with a perfect heart. The Lord promises healing to those who "diligently hearken to the voice of the Lord…and…do that which is right in His sight" (Exodus 15:20).

As believers in Christ, we do not plead our own righteousness but the righteousness of Him who "was wounded for our transgressions… bruised for our iniquities" and with whose stripes "we are healed" (Isaiah 53:5; Matthew 8:16–17).

---

[35] See Psalm 18:36 and Psalm 119:105

[36] See Isaiah 43:26; Hosea 14:2

[37] See Isaiah 38:1–8

When multiple armies rose up against Jehoshaphat, he set Israel to fast and pray. In his prayer, he put God in remembrance of His Word to them. Israel won that battle without throwing a punch. God Himself fought for them. He caused the enemy to fight against themselves and destroy themselves.[38]

Taking God's Word back to Him demonstrates faith in Him. You are telling Him that He is in control, that it is His will that should be done, not yours. God will *always* honor His Word.

We are to follow our Shepherd in total faith and obedience in order to enjoy green pastures. He is the Shepherd and there is no one else.

Total faith and obedience require a surrendered and humble heart. That is how Jesus fulfilled His ministry: in total obedience to His Father and with a perfectly humble heart.[39]

---

[38] 2 Chronicles 20

[39] See John 6:38 and Philippians 2:5–8

Chapter Five

CONSECRATION
AND FELLOWSHIP

Thou preparest a table before me in the presence of mine enemies:
Thou anointest my head with oil my cup runneth over.

—PSALM 23:5

THE COMMUNION

It is the Lord Himself who prepares the table. He knows exactly
what we need and at what particular time. The Bible tells us that the
mercies and compassion of the Lord are new every morning. That
should bring great comfort to the believer because it means that God
knows what we need for each day and what we will face each day, and
makes those provisions for us every day. We do not have to depend on
the victory of yesterday. He provides new mercies, new strength, new
victories, and new comfort, according to our several needs each day.

We do not even have to think about how we are going to go through a day because He already has every need met and ready for us.

O the depth of God's love and grace to us. All we need to do is trust Him with every aspect of our lives.

The Lord allowed the enemies to be around, but they are powerless against His sheep, because Jesus "spoilt principalities and powers" (Colossians 2:15) on our behalf. The Greek word used here is *apekduomai* and it means to strip off, disarm, or take off completely. Principalities and powers were stripped of their authority over God's children by Jesus Christ our Lord.

We are still in the world, but we are not under the rule of the world's system whose premise is sin. This does not mean a free pass for anarchy and civil disobedience. The Bible warns against that in 1 Peter 2:13–17.

In John 17:15, Jesus prays to the Father that we should not be taken out of the world, but rather be kept from the evil in it.

We sit at the table prepared by the Lord, and we feast on the good things He has given us, which is everything that pertains to life and godliness according to 2 Peter 1:3–4. Verse 3 tells us also that this life, which is God's own life, and godliness are only obtained through the knowledge of Jesus Christ. Second Peter 1:4 reveals that to know Jesus more is to know more of what God has provided for us through Him. The only reason we are even invited to sit at the table is because Jesus is our Shepherd and Lord. We are then obligated to seek to know Him more. When we hunger and thirst for Him, the Holy Spirit brings revelation of Him in our hearts through His Word.[40]

---

[40] See John 16:13–14

THE ANOINTING

Dining at the Lord's table means fellowship with Him. It is communion.

Here is a believer walking unafraid through the valley of the shadow of death, so focused on the Lord he cares not what dangers are lurking around him. He eventually gets to fellowship with the Lord at His own table. There, in the presence of the Lord during fellowship, the Lord anoints him with oil, the oil of His Holy Spirit that soothes, heals, comforts, calms, and empowers.[41] Sometimes Christians talk of the anointing as if it is something you purchase from a bookstore.

Take note that the anointing is experienced only at the table of the Lord.

When someone is invited to lunch or dinner by a friend, that person does not take a quick look around on arrival, pick up just those items he or she likes, and then walk away without sitting down to eat. That would be extremely rude and an insult to one's host. However, we behave like that with God, who has invited us to dine at His table. Sharing a meal is fellowship and forges a bond.[42] If we are honest, many of us would admit that we do not fellowship with God as He would like us to. For some of us, even five minutes of prayer is a burden. If we do go beyond five minutes, we simply tabulate all that God is supposed to do for us and do not take the time to hear from Him. We do not take time to sit with Him, to eat and drink from His Word, and allow Him to show us great and marvelous things that we did not know before.[43]

---

[41] Isaiah 61:3; Psalm 89:20–23

[42] See Acts 2:46–47

[43] See Jeremiah 33:3

This is how we miss out on the anointing, through which God empowers us to live as He wants us to.[44] Then we wonder why we are not experiencing the victory God has promised us. We need the anointing of God daily for daily victory. When the Lord anoints us, our cups run over and there is an outward manifestation of that inner work of grace. We can resist temptation, stand in faith, and, like Paul, can genuinely say, "I can do all things through Christ who strengthens me" (Philippians 4:13). This is God's strength being made perfect in us.[45]

It is by the anointing that the yoke is broken: "It is not by might nor by power, but by My Spirit says the Lord of hosts" (Zechariah 4:6).

Yokes are not broken as a result of our gifts of oratory, or our knowledge of particular subjects, or our perfect form of presentation. All these are okay to have in the secular world, but when it comes to God's Kingdom's business, that work is exclusively achieved by God Himself.

The apostles were not just waiting on the Lord for the power of the Holy Ghost that Jesus promised. They were waiting in prayer—daily. They kept themselves at the Lord's table daily in prayer and supplication until the Spirit was poured upon them from on high.[46]

Even though these men had walked and lived in the presence of Jesus, they still had to obey the invitation to come and dine in His presence. Jesus had instructed them "tarry in the city of Jerusalem until you are endued with power from on high" (Luke 24:49)—and they did.

---

[44] See 1 John 2:27

[45] See 2 Corinthians 12:9

[46] Acts 2

After the Holy Spirit had filled them, we see a great transformation in these men who had been following Jesus, but who after His death became very fearful and went back to their original occupations.[47]

We see Peter, who had denied Jesus to the point of swearing untrue oaths, become the leader and orator God had intended him to be.[48] We see those same men who had been in hiding for fear of their lives display such boldness that the Jewish rulers of their day were baffled.[49] The rulers came to the conclusion that the power they were seeing manifested in the apostles was because they had been with Jesus. What a testimony, and it is all the more miraculous because these apostles were simple, uneducated men. They had no formal education, but they stumped the learned rulers.

It is by the anointing that every yoke is broken, not by might or by power according to the Word of the Lord.

As believers in Christ, we need that enabling power that only the Holy Spirit gives. We can only receive it as we stay in His presence.

Jesus Himself showed us that same example of staying in the presence of His Father when He was here on earth. He always took time out to pray and commune with His Father.

He took time out—forty days—before He began His earthly ministry. At the end of those forty days the Bible tells us that He returned to Galilee "in the power of the Spirit" (Luke 4:14). After that, Jesus began His ministry.

He took time out in the middle of His ministry to be refreshed.[50]

---

[47] See John 21:2–4

[48] See Matthew 26:74

[49] See Acts 4:18–31

[50] See Luke 5:16

He also took time out before making major decisions.[51] It was after the all-night prayer on the mountain that He chose His twelve disciples.

We all know that faced with the prospect of the cross, Jesus prayed earnestly; He was strengthened and was able to be obedient unto the death on the cross.[52]

Every one of Jesus's actions is an example for us to follow. Let us be obedient to His calling to dine with Him and be refreshed and empowered. Remember He is the Restorer of our souls; He replenishes our energy when we are spent.

He does the work of grace in our hearts to do His will by the anointing of the Holy Ghost.

The Lord told Saul, the first King of Israel,

> "And the Spirit of the LORD will come upon thee, and thou shalt prophesy with them, and shalt be turned into another man. And let it be, that when these signs are come unto thee, that thou do as occasion serve thee; for God is with thee." (1 Samuel 10:6–7)

Let us therefore not neglect to continually sit at His table, to which we have been invited and where we are always welcome, and bask in His Presence, His power, and His anointing.

---

[51] See Luke 6:12–16

[52] See Luke 22:41–46

Chapter Six

CONFIDENCE IN THE LORD

Surely goodness and mercy shall follow me all the days of my life: and I will dwell in the house of the Lord for ever.

—PSALM 23:6

After enumerating all that the Shepherd does for him, the psalmist concludes by affirming that such goodness and mercy will never fail him. It is forever. Whatsoever God does is forever.[53] That is the hope that Jesus gave us in John14:1–3. Goodness and mercy are in the presence of God and, if we continue in them, we will continue in His presence.[54]

He uses the word *surely* to affirm his faith in God's goodness and

---

[53] Ecclesiastes 3:14

[54] Revelation 21:1–4 and 22:1–5; Psalm16:11

mercy. He is totally convinced of those two things: God's goodness and God's mercy.

FULLY PERSUADED

The Bible exhorts us to be fully persuaded in our hearts of our faith in Christ.[55] We must be fully persuaded in our hearts of the goodness of God. Otherwise, we will not be able trust Him at all. We would always be in doubt about God's will for us. He assures in Jeremiah 29:11 that His thoughts toward us are continually of peace, not of evil, to give us an expected end. Even though the Lord was here speaking specifically to the Israelites in captivity in Babylon, that word and promise is for us also who believe in Him through His Son Jesus Christ our Lord, our Savior and our Shepherd.

This affirmation is both a confession of faith in God's everlasting covenant of mercy and grace and of the psalmist's own willingness to follow the Good Shepherd all the way.

He knows the way. He led the children of Israel through the wilderness by going before them.[56] The LORD knows the dangers that are in the way as we journey through life. Jesus has gone before us and cleared the way for us by spoiling principalities and powers on the cross.[57] Now we can follow Him in full confidence that He has defeated our foes already and He is still with us wherever we go.

We must also be fully persuaded of God's mercy. I once heard someone ask this question during one of our Bible studies: "Why does God punish His children?" To that person, it seemed like those

---

[55] Romans 14:5

[56] Exodus 13:21–22; Deuteronomy 31:8

[57] Colossians 2:15

who are not God's children were having a better deal in this world than God's own children. Unbelievers seem to prosper more and face less calamities.

This is the same dilemma that faced David as he was contemplating God's goodness and mercy in Psalm 73. He was disturbed at the thought that the unrighteous seemed to be so much more prosperous than the children of God.[58] It was in his heart for some time; he mulled over it and was greatly disturbed by it. He felt that leading a righteous life was pointless and that caused him so much pain.[59] He felt that way until he sought the LORD, and then he was able to understand certain things:

1. That the unrepentant unrighteous have already been judged by the LORD; and
2. Their end of destruction has already been determined by the LORD.

When David finally understood, he repented of the sin of doubt and unbelief. We see this in verses 21 and 22 of this psalm. He was then able to say, "My flesh and heart faileth: but God is the strength of my heart, and my portion for ever" (Psalm 73:26).

This means that even though he went through difficulties and trials, he is assured that God is with him always. He is assured of God's restoration, he is assured of God's strength, and he is assured of God's presence.

In 2 Thessalonians, we are exhorted to be patient and faithful in the face of suffering and tribulations that might come our way.

---

[58] See verses 2 through 12
[59] See verses 13 through 16

This is so we may be counted worthy of His kingdom.[60] God has a purpose for every trial that comes our way: to strengthen our faith and make us worthy of His kingdom.

He allowed the Israelites to go through the "scenic" route in the wilderness to test their faith in Him. He wanted them to see and know how much He loved them and the greatness of His power towards them.[61] Unfortunately all the children of Israel saw were the hardships in the wilderness. They forgot all the mighty works He did for them at their every point of need.[62] The Word tells us that even though the Israelites saw the wonders of God, which was the gospel being preached to them, not all of them had faith in what they had heard and seen.[63] Therefore, they could not and did not enter into the Lord's rest because of their unbelief.

However, those who continue to believe in God's goodness, mercy, and power despite trials and difficulties will enter into that rest, which is the Kingdom of God.

That is the rest that only Jesus gives because He is our Rest.

Jesus once told His disciples, "And from the days of John the Baptist until now the Kingdom of God suffereth violence and the violent take it by force" (Matthew 11:12).

This means that every proclamation of faith in Christ will be tested. We are in a battle, and Jesus assured us that we shall have tribulations in the world but peace in Him.[64] No matter the trials, we are assured of victory in Him. We have to always be sober and

---

[60] Verses 4 and 5

[61] See Isaiah 43:12 and 21

[62] Deuteronomy 8:2–6

[63] See Hebrews 4:2

[64] John 16:33

vigilant as we are exhorted to in 1 Peter 3:8–9. We have an adversary who has already been defeated, but he is still going about looking for those whose faith is weak so he can devour them. We are exhorted to resist the devil steadfastly in faith. We should be able to say, "The LORD is on my side; I will not fear" (Psalm 118:6–7) and "Though I walk through the valley of the shadow of death, I will fear no evil" (Psalm 23:4).

Though I walk through the fire, I will not fear.[65] We will we not fear because we know that the LORD is good and His mercy endures forever.

Job was so convinced of God's goodness and mercy, in spite of all his trials, that he testified with absolute faith that he knew that God's purpose was to refine him as gold at the end of it all.[66] That is exactly God's purpose for each of His children: to be conformed to the image of His dear Son Jesus (Romans 8:29).

In Christ, we will dwell in the House of the Lord forever because "Whatsoever God doeth, it shall be forever" (Ecclesiastes 3:14).

He is the eternal God, His kingdom is everlasting and because He is Life, we have eternal life in Christ.

May this always be our testimony: that God has given us eternal life and this life is in His Son (John 5:11) so shall we dwell in the house of the Lord forever.

---

[65] See Isaiah 43:2
[66] Job 23:10

Printed in the United States
by Baker & Taylor Publisher Services